"The only person you are destined to become is the person you decide to be."

— Ralph Waldo Emerson

MAN MOVES

YOUR NEXT VERSION WILL
BE YOUR BEST VERSION

AARON L. HOUSTON

To the Men of Purpose,

This book is dedicated to you—men of strength, resilience, and untapped potential. It is dedicated to the dreamers, the warriors, and the seekers of truth who dare to envision a life of purpose and meaning.

To the ones who refuse to settle for mediocrity and strive relentlessly for excellence in every aspect of their lives.

To fathers, sons, brothers, and friends who understand the power of vulnerability, the beauty of authenticity, and the significance of standing firm in their convictions.

May the words within these pages ignite a fire within you—a fire to pursue your dreams with unwavering determination, face your fears with courage and grace, and embrace the journey of becoming the best version of yourself.

May you find inspiration, encouragement, and wisdom to navigate life's challenges, overcome obstacles, and emerge victorious in the pursuit of your God-given destiny.

This book is dedicated to you, dear sir, with the utmost respect and admiration for the incredible journey that lies ahead.

Here is to your growth, your maturity, and your relentless pursuit of greatness.

With deep appreciation and anticipation for the journey ahead.

Aaron L. Houston

TABLE OF CONTENTS

Dear Reader,

Welcome to a journey of transformation. In these pages, I share insights gleaned from my own journey—a path marked by triumphs, trials, and lessons learned.

This book serves as a roadmap for navigating the complexities of manhood, offering stories of courage, principles for living with purpose, and encouragement for pursuing your passions.

Approach these words with an open mind and heart. Let them challenge, stretch, and inspire you to rise above the ordinary and embrace the extraordinary calling in your life.

Remember, you are not alone. There is a community of men walking alongside you, ready to support and uplift you.

So, dive in, explore, and engage with the ideas presented here. May this book ignite a fire within you—a fire to pursue your dreams, live with integrity, and become the man you were created to be.

With anticipation for the journey ahead.

Aaron L. Houston

INTRODUCTION

In a world filled with distractions, demands, and doubts, it is easy for men to lose sight of who they are and what they were created to be. We live in a culture that often confuses strength with aggression, success with status, and masculinity with machismo. But deep within each of us lies a longing—a desire to live a life of purpose, integrity, and impact.

It is this longing that has brought you to these pages. Whether you are seeking guidance, inspiration, or simply a sense of camaraderie, know that you are in good company. For I, too, have felt the tug of that inner longing—the call to rise above the noise and chaos of everyday life and discover what it truly means to be a man of God.

In this book, we are going on a journey—a journey of discovery, growth, and transformation. Together, we will explore the timeless truths of the Scripture, uncovering insights that have the power to reshape our thinking, our actions, and our very lives. We will delve into topics ranging from leadership and integrity to relationships and purpose, seeking wisdom for the challenges we face and the dreams we pursue.

But more than just a book of ideas, this is a call to action—a challenge to step out of the shadows of complacency and embrace the fullness of who God created us to be. It is a reminder that we are called to live with courage, compassion, and conviction—to be men who lead with humility, love with sincerity, and serve with selflessness.

So, my friend, join me on this journey; open your heart, your mind, and your hands to receive the blessings that await. May this book be a guide, a companion, and a source of strength as you navigate the adventure of life and embrace the fullness of your God-given potential.

With anticipation for the journey ahead.

Aaron L. Houston

CHAPTER 1

RISE OF THE WARRIOR SPIRIT:
EMBRACING YOUR DIVINE PURPOSE

To every man reading this book of insight and inspiration, let me begin by saying that amidst all the chaos and conflict in this huge universe, there still exists a divine purpose for your life. It is a purpose that transcends the mundane, the trivial, and the fleeting desires of this world. It is a purpose that ignites the flames of the warrior spirit within, calling forth courage, strength, and resilience in the face of adversity. It is a purpose that resonates with the heartbeat of creation itself, pulsating with the rhythm of destiny. It is not by chance that this book has found its way into your hands, and the hope is that the contents will find its way into your head and flow into your heart.

As men, we are called to rise above the noise of the world and embrace our divine purpose with unwavering resolve. We are called to embody the essence of the warrior spirit, to stand firm in our convictions, and to march boldly into the battlefield of life. For it is in the crucible of challenge and conflict that our true strength is forged. It is through the pursuit of our purpose that we find meaning and fulfillment in this journey called life.

But what is this divine purpose that is calling us forth? That is indeed a question that has echoed through the ages, whispered in the depths of our souls, and is found in the depths of our DNA. It is a question that each man must answer for himself, for it is a journey of self-discovery and revelation.

Our divine purpose is not a destination to be reached but a journey to be embraced. It is not a static state of being but a dynamic process of personal research and development, growth, and transformation. It is the realization that we are more than the sum of our parts, more than the roles we play or the seasonal masks we wear. It is the recognition that we are not humans having a series of spiritual experiences but rather spiritual beings having a series of human experiences in a single lifetime. We are called to transcend the limitations of our physical existence and tap into the infinite wellspring of divine wisdom and power that lies within.

To embrace our divine purpose is to align ourselves with the will of our Majestic Creator, abandon our egotistical desires and self-centered ambitions, and surrender ourselves to the greater good of all. It is to recognize that we are not separate from the world around us but, in this very space and time, connected to it in a web of interdependence and mutual co-creation.

The rise of the warrior spirit begins with a deep inner knowing, a primal intuition that stirs within the depths of our being. It is a call to arms, a call to awaken from the slumber of complacency and mediocrity. It is a piercing and deafening call to rise to the challenge of greatness. It is a command to step into our power, harness the full force of our purpose and potential, and ultimately unleash our creative genius upon the world.

But this journey is not for the faint-hearted, nor is it for the timid or the weak-willed. It is a journey of courage and conviction, of perseverance and resilience. It is a journey that will test us to our very core, pushing us to the brink of our limits and beyond. Yet it is also a journey of immense beauty and wonder, allure and refinement, discovery and revelation.

It will be in this divine pursuit of our divine purpose that we will discover the true essence of who we are—warriors of light, champions of truth, and vessels of divine love. We will discover that our strength lies not in the might of our sword or the power of our fist but in the depth of our character and the purity of our heart. We will discover that our purpose is not to conquer and dominate but to serve and uplift, to inspire and empower, and to leave a legacy of love and inspiration that will reverberate for generations to come.

As we journey forth into the unknown, let us remember that we do not walk alone. For we are surrounded by a great cloud of witnesses—the souls of the wise and the brave who have gone before us, blazing a trail of light across the annals of history. Let us draw strength from their example, courage from their bravery, and inspiration from their legacy.

And so, hear me well, my mighty brothers, let us rise together—as warriors of the light, as champions of truth, and as vessels of divine love. Let us embrace our divine purpose with unwavering resolve, knowing that we are called to absolutely nothing less than greatness. For in the words of the ancient sage, "The greatest glory in living lies not in never falling, but in rising every time we fall."

CHAPTER 2

FORGING STRENGTH THROUGH ADVERSITY:
OVERCOMING LIFE'S CHALLENGES

The mighty blacksmith's fire is continuously used to shape and temper the raw materials of our character. Contrary to many popular beliefs, it is through the trials and tribulations that we encounter along our journey that we are forged into beings of strength, resilience, and unwavering resolve. Adversity, far from being a hindrance, can usually be the very catalyst for our growth and transformation.

Life's challenges come in various shapes and sizes, each presenting its own unique set of obstacles and opportunities for growth. Whether it be the loss of a loved one, the failure of a dream, or the pain of a broken relationship, adversity has its own special way of testing the very fabric of our being, pushing us to the brink of despair, desperation, and sometimes even death.

Yet, it is in the face of adversity that our true strength is revealed. It is in those moments of darkness and despair that we discover the depth of our resilience, the power of our will, and the tenacity of our spirit, for it is easy to be strong when the sun is shining, and the winds are at our back, but it is in the midst of madness and the lunacy of life's storms that our true strength is put to the test.

One of the greatest lessons that adversity teaches us is the importance of perseverance. In the face of seemingly insurmountable odds, it is our ability to keep going and to keep pushing forward that ultimately leads to victory. As the saying goes, "When you're going through hell, keep going." It is in the act of putting one foot in front of the other, day after day that we find the strength to overcome even the greatest of obstacles.

But perseverance alone is not enough. We must also cultivate resilience—the ability to bounce back from adversity stronger and more determined than ever before. Resilience is not about avoiding hardship or pain but about embracing it fully and allowing it to shape us into beings of greater strength and wisdom. Resilience is a trait that gives us the strength to handle unavoidable inconveniences and inevitable hardships.

One of the keys to building resilience is the practice of gratitude. In the midst of our darkest moments, it can be extremely easy to focus on what we have lost or what we lack.

However, true resilience comes from shifting our focus to what we still have and what remains. True resilience reminds us of the blessings and opportunities that surround us, even amid adversity. By cultivating an attitude of gratitude, we are able to find hope and strength even in the darkest and most dismal of times.

Another key to building resilience is the power of perspective. The particular way a person understands or views something is a simple definition of perspective. While wrestling with adversity, it can be easy to lose sight of the bigger picture and become consumed by our own pain and suffering. But by stepping back and taking a broader view of our situation, we can see that even the greatest challenges are temporary and that every setback is an opportunity for growth and transformation. Positive perspectives can be challenging to come about at times of hurt and life's harassment, but it can happen.

Ultimately, the journey through adversity is a journey of self-discovery and transformation. It is a journey that tests us to our very core, pushing us to the brink of our limits and, oftentimes, beyond. But it is also a journey that holds the promise of great reward—the reward of greater strength, deeper wisdom, and a renewed sense of purpose and meaning.

As we navigate the storms of life, let us remember that adversity is not our enemy but our greatest teacher. Sometimes, it whispers. Sometimes, it howls. But every chance it gets, adversity will teach us something if we are open and desire to learn. Through the fires of adversity, we are forged into beings of strength, resilience, and unwavering resolve. And it is through overcoming life's challenges that we discover the true depth of our courage, the power of our will, and the boundless potential of our spirit.

CHAPTER 3

THE ANATOMY OF LEADERSHIP:
CULTIVATING INFLUENCE AND IMPACT

One thing I have learned on my personal journey is that leadership must be able to stand as the bold and vibrant banner that it is. If leadership was a thread, you must allow it to weave its way through the fabric of your human experience. You have to allow it to be a guiding force that inspires, motivates, encourages, and empowers others to reach their full potential.

Leadership, in its essence, is not merely about holding a position of authority or wielding power over others. It is about service, influence, and the ability to bring about positive change in a world that so desperately needs it.

As men called to lead, we must understand the intricacies and anatomy of leadership—the qualities and characteristics that set great leaders apart from the not-so-great leaders or those who may not be leading at all. We must cultivate these qualities within ourselves, nurturing them with care and intentionality so that we may become vessels of influence and impact in every single corner of our universe and every arc of our spheres of influence.

One of the foundational qualities of leadership is vision. Proverbs 29:18 reminds us, "Where there is no vision, the people perish." A leader without a clear vision is like a ship without a rudder, drifting aimlessly on the seas of uncertainty. It is the leader's responsibility to cast a compelling vision for the future, to inspire others to join in the pursuit of a common goal and to chart a course of success towards that vision with unwavering determination.

But please hear me well; vision alone is not enough. A true leader must also possess the ability to communicate that vision effectively. Proverbs 18:21 tells us, "The tongue has the power of life and death, and those who love it will eat its fruit." Through the power of words, a leader is able to inspire, motivate, and, probably more importantly, mobilize others to action. By painting a vivid picture of the desired future and articulating a clear plan for achieving it, a leader can rally the collective efforts of those around him towards a common purpose.

Yet, leadership is not merely about giving orders or barking commands. It is about serving others with humility and compassion. In Mark 10:45, Jesus himself exemplifies this principle, saying, "For even the Son of Man did not come to be served, but to serve, and to give his life as a ransom for many." A true leader leads by example, rolling up his sleeves and getting his hands dirty alongside those he leads. He listens with empathy, seeks to understand the needs and concerns of others, and works tirelessly to support and uplift those under his care.

Another essential quality of leadership is integrity. Proverbs 11:3 declares, "The integrity of the upright guides them, but the unfaithful are destroyed by their duplicity." A leader who lacks integrity is like a house built on sand, destined to crumble at the slightest breeze. Integrity is the bedrock upon which trust is built, and trust is the currency of leadership. A leader who consistently acts with honesty, transparency, and moral courage earns the respect and loyalty of those he leads.

The anatomy of leadership can be described as a series of multifaceted moments of vision, communication, service, and integrity. As men called to lead, we must strive to cultivate these qualities within ourselves, knowing that we have leadership leverage that could impact and extend far beyond our immediate spheres of influence. Let us heed the words of 1 Timothy 4:12, which says, "Don't let anyone look down on you because you are young, but set an example for the believers in speech, in conduct, in love, in faith and in purity." Let us rise to the challenge of leadership with humility, courage, and unwavering commitment, knowing that the world is in desperate need of leaders who lead with vision, compassion, and integrity.

CHAPTER 4

MASTERING THE ART OF SELF-DISCIPLINE:
HARNESSING YOUR INNER POWER

In the grand symphony of life, self-discipline stands as the conductor, orchestrating the harmonious rhythm of our actions and decisions. It is the guiding force that propels us towards our goals and aspirations, even in the face of temptation and adversity. Self-discipline, far from being a tyrant or oppressor, is the key to unlocking our full potential and achieving lasting success and fulfillment.

As men striving to fulfill our divine purpose, we must understand the importance of mastering the art of self-discipline. It is the cornerstone upon which all other virtues are built, the foundation upon which our dreams and aspirations take flight.

Without self-discipline, our goals remain nothing more than lofty aspirations, forever out of reach.

The Bible speaks extensively on the topic of self-discipline, recognizing its central role in the life of the believer. In 1 Corinthians 9:27, the Apostle Paul writes, "I discipline my body like an athlete, training it to do what it should. Otherwise, I fear that after preaching to others, I myself might be disqualified." Paul understood that self-discipline is not a one-time event but a daily practice, requiring constant effort and vigilance.

So, how do we go about mastering the art of self-discipline? It begins with the cultivation of self-awareness—the ability to recognize our weaknesses and temptations and to develop strategies for overcoming them. In Proverbs 4:23, we are admonished to "Above all else, guard your heart, for everything you do flows from it." By guarding our hearts and minds against negative influences and distractions, we can cultivate the inner strength and resilience needed to resist temptation and stay focused on our goals.

Another key aspect of mastering self-discipline is the establishment of healthy habits and routines. In Joshua 1:8, God instructs Joshua, "Keep this Book of the Law always on your lips; meditate on it day and night, so that you may be careful to do everything written in it. Then you will be prosperous and successful." By incorporating daily practices such as prayer, meditation, and reflection into our lives, we can strengthen our spiritual muscles and develop the discipline needed to overcome life's challenges.

But self-discipline is not just about saying no to temptation; it is also about saying yes to the things that matter most. In Philippians 4:13, Paul declares, "I can do all things through Christ who strengthens me." By aligning our goals and aspirations with God's will for our lives, we tap into a source of strength and power that transcends our own human limitations. It is through the power of God's grace working within us that we are able to overcome our weaknesses and achieve our full potential.

Mastering the art of self-discipline is a lifelong journey requiring patience, perseverance, and unwavering commitment. But the rewards far outweigh the challenges. By harnessing the power of self-discipline, we can overcome any obstacle, achieve any goal, and fulfill our divine purpose in this world. Let us heed the words of Hebrews 12:11, which says, "No discipline seems pleasant at the time, but painful. Later on, however, it produces a harvest of righteousness and peace for those who have been trained by it." Let us embrace the discipline of self-discipline with joy and gratitude, knowing that it is the key to unlocking our full potential and living a life of purpose and fulfillment.

CHAPTER 5

UNLEASHING THE POWER OF VISION:
CRAFTING YOUR PATH TO SUCCESS

In this blessed gift that we call life, vision stands as the guiding star, illuminating the path to our greatest dreams and aspirations. It is the beacon of light that leads us out of the darkness of uncertainty and into the brilliance of possibility. Vision, far from being a fleeting fantasy or idle daydream, is the catalyst for transformation and a vital key to unlocking our full potential.

As men called to greatness, we must understand the power of vision and its role in shaping our destiny. For without a clear vision of where we are going, we are like ships adrift on the sea of life, at the mercy of the winds and currents of circumstance. But with a compelling vision to guide us, we become captains of our own fate, charting a course towards our desired destination with confidence and purpose.

The Bible is replete with examples of men and women who dared to dream big and pursue their vision with unwavering faith and determination. In Genesis 15:5, God promises Abraham, "Look up at the sky and count the stars—if indeed you can count them. So shall your offspring be." Despite his advanced age and the apparent impossibility of the promise, Abraham chose to believe in the vision that God had given him, and as a result, he became the Father of nations.

So, how do we go about unleashing the power of vision in our own lives? It begins with clarity—a clear and compelling picture of what we want to achieve and who we want to become. In Proverbs 29:18, we are reminded, "Where there is no vision, the people perish." Without a clear vision to guide us, we are prone to wander aimlessly through life, never fully realizing our potential or fulfilling our divine purpose.

But clarity alone is not enough. We must also possess the courage to pursue our vision with unwavering faith and determination, even in the face of opposition and adversity. In Joshua 1:9, God commands Joshua, "Be strong and courageous. Do not be afraid; do not be discouraged, for the Lord your God will be with you wherever you go." By stepping out in faith and taking bold action toward our vision, we demonstrate our trust in God's provision and faithfulness.

Another key aspect of unleashing the power of vision is the practice of visualization—the act of mentally rehearsing our desired outcomes and experiencing them as if they were already reality. In Habakkuk 2:2, God instructs the prophet, "Write down the vision and make it plain on tablets, that he may run who reads it." By visualizing our goals and aspirations with clarity and intensity, we align our thoughts, emotions, and actions with the realization of our vision.

Unleashing the power of vision is a transformative journey that requires clarity, courage, and unwavering faith. By crafting a clear and compelling vision for our lives and pursuing it with passion and purpose, we can overcome any obstacle, achieve any goal, and fulfill our divine destiny. Let us heed the words of Proverbs 16:3, which says, "Commit to the Lord whatever you do, and he will establish your plans." Let us commit our vision to the Lord and trust in his provision and guidance as we journey towards our greatest dreams and aspirations.

CHAPTER 6

THE COURAGE TO CONQUER FEAR:
STEPPING INTO BOLDNESS AND CONFIDENCE

Fear can be a frightful force to contend with. No one asks for it or desires it, but at some point, we will all have to deal with it. Fear stands as the shadowy adversary, casting doubt and uncertainty upon our path and doing its best to prevent us from moving forward. It is the whispering voice that seeks to paralyze us with doubt and rob us of our purpose and potential. Yet, as men called to greatness, we are tasked with the courageous act of stepping boldly into the face of fear, armed with confidence and determination.

The Bible is filled with admonitions to fear not, for God is with us. Consider Psalm 27:1, a verse that speaks directly to the spirit of fear, "The Lord is my light and my salvation—whom shall I fear?" Fear will manifest, but as men, we will manage. In Isaiah 41:10, we are reminded, "Fear not, for I am with you; be not dismayed, for I am your God; I will strengthen you, I will help you, I will uphold you with my righteous right hand." This assurance of divine presence gives us the courage to confront our fears head-on, knowing that we do not face them alone.

But conquering fear requires more than just faith; it requires action. In Joshua 1:9, God commands Joshua, "Be strong and courageous. Do not be frightened, and do not be dismayed, for the Lord your God is with you wherever you go." By taking bold and decisive action in the face of fear, we demonstrate our trust in God's provision and our commitment to fulfilling our divine purpose.

One of the most powerful antidotes to fear is confidence—a deep-seated belief in our own abilities and the certainty of our ultimate success. In Philippians 4:13, the Apostle Paul declares, "I can do all things through him who strengthens me." By tapping into the power of God working within us, we can overcome any obstacle and achieve our greatest dreams and aspirations.

However, confidence is not something that we are born with; it is something that we must cultivate through deliberate practice and positive reinforcement. In Romans 12:2, Paul exhorts us, "Do not be conformed to this world, but be transformed by the renewal of your mind, that by testing you may discern what the will of God is, what is good and acceptable and perfect." By renewing our minds with positive affirmations and empowering beliefs, we can build the confidence needed to conquer fear and step boldly into our destiny.

Another key aspect of conquering fear is the practice of courage—the willingness to take risks and step outside of our comfort zone in pursuit of our goals and aspirations. In 2 Timothy 1:7, Paul reminds us, "For God gave us a spirit not of fear but of power and love and self-control." By embracing the spirit of courage within us, we can overcome the paralyzing grip of fear and unleash our full potential.

The courage to conquer fear is not a one-time event but a lifelong journey of growth and transformation. By cultivating faith, confidence, and courage within ourselves, we can overcome any obstacle, achieve any goal, and fulfill our divine purpose in this world. Let us heed the words of Psalm 27:1, which says, "The Lord is my light and my salvation; whom shall I fear? The Lord is the stronghold of my life; of whom shall I be afraid?" Let us stand firm in the knowledge that we are children of the Most High God, called to walk in boldness and confidence as we journey towards our greatest dreams and aspirations.

CHAPTER 7

NAVIGATING RELATIONSHIPS:

HONORING YOUR ROLE AS PROTECTOR AND PROVIDER

Our relationships can arguably be considered to be one of the more important cornerstones of our lives, forming the very foundation upon which we build our lives and livelihoods. They are the bonds that connect us, the source of love, support, and companionship that sustains us through life's ups and downs. As men called to greatness, we are tasked with the sacred duty of navigating relationships with wisdom, integrity, and grace, honoring our role as protectors and providers.

The Bible is rich with wisdom on the subject of relationships, offering guidance on how to cultivate healthy and fulfilling connections with those around us. In Ephesians 5:25, husbands are instructed to love their wives as Christ loved the church, sacrificing themselves for their wives' sake. This admonition speaks to the importance of selflessness and sacrifice in our relationships, recognizing that true love is not self-serving but self-giving.

As protectors and providers, it is our responsibility to create a safe and nurturing environment in which our loved ones can flourish and thrive. In 1 Timothy 5:8, Paul writes, "But if anyone does not provide for his relatives, and especially for members of his household, he has denied the faith and is worse than an unbeliever." This verse underscores the importance of providing for the physical, emotional, and spiritual needs of our families, ensuring that they are well cared for and supported in every way.

Our role as protectors and providers extends beyond our immediate family to encompass all those within our sphere of influence. In Luke 10:27, Jesus commands us to love our neighbors as ourselves, showing kindness and compassion to all those we encounter. This principle reminds us that we are called to be a source of blessing and encouragement to those around us, using our resources and influence for the betterment of others.

One of the key aspects of navigating relationships is communication—the ability to listen with empathy, speak with honesty, and resolve conflicts with grace. In Proverbs 18:13, we are reminded, "If one gives an answer before he hears, it is his folly and shame." By practicing active listening and seeking to understand the perspectives and feelings of others, we can build deeper connections and foster greater intimacy in our relationships.

An essential aspect of navigating relationships is humility—the willingness to admit when we are wrong, ask for forgiveness, and extend grace to others. In Philippians 2:3-4, Paul exhorts us, "Do nothing from selfish ambition or conceit, but in humility count others more significant than yourselves. Let each of you look not only to his own interests but also to the interests of others." By putting the needs and interests of others above our own, we demonstrate Christ-like love and humility in our relationships.

Navigating relationships is a sacred and noble calling, requiring wisdom, humility, and selflessness. As men called to greatness, let us honor our role as protectors and providers, creating a safe and nurturing environment in which our loved ones can flourish and thrive. Let us heed the words of 1 Peter 4:8, which says, "Above all, keep loving one another earnestly, since love covers a multitude of sins." Let us love one another with sincerity and devotion, knowing that in doing so, we fulfill our divine purpose and bring glory to God.

CHAPTER 8

FATHERHOOD:

EMBRACING THE SACRED RESPONSIBILITY OF GUIDING GENERATIONS

To be a father is a huge blessing, and fatherhood stands as a supreme and sacred calling. A divine appointment entrusted to us by the Creator Himself. Fatherhood is a role of profound significance and responsibility, requiring wisdom, strength, and unwavering commitment. As men called to greatness, we are tasked with the sacred duty of guiding and shaping the next generation, instilling within them the values, virtues, and vision needed to thrive in a world filled with challenges and opportunities.

The Bible offers timeless wisdom on the subject of fatherhood, providing guidance on how to fulfill this sacred responsibility with grace and integrity. In Proverbs 22:6, we are instructed to "Train up a child in the way he should go; even when he is old, he will not depart from it." This verse underscores the importance of teaching and modeling righteousness, integrity, and wisdom for our children, laying a firm foundation upon which they can build their lives.

As fathers, we are called to be role models and mentors, leading by example and imparting wisdom through both our words and our actions. In Deuteronomy 6:6-7, we are commanded, "And these words that I command you today shall be on your heart. You shall teach them diligently to your children and shall talk of them when you sit in your house, and when you walk by the way, and when you lie down, and when you rise." This passage emphasizes the importance of integrating faith and values into every aspect of our daily lives so that our children may see and emulate our commitment to righteousness and integrity.

However, fatherhood is not just about imparting knowledge; it is also about nurturing and affirming the unique gifts and talents of each child. In Psalm 127:3, we are reminded, "Behold, children are a heritage from the Lord, the fruit of the womb a reward." Each child is a precious gift from God, endowed with their own strengths, passions, and potential. As fathers, it is our responsibility to cultivate and nurture these gifts, helping our children discover their purpose and pursue their dreams with confidence and determination.

One of the greatest challenges of fatherhood is providing a safe and nurturing environment in which our children can flourish and thrive. In Ephesians 6:4, fathers are admonished, "Fathers, do not provoke your children to anger, but bring them up in the discipline and instruction of the Lord." This verse speaks to the importance of setting boundaries and providing structure and discipline for our children while also offering them love, encouragement, and support.

But perhaps the greatest gift that we can give to our children is the gift of presence—being fully engaged and emotionally available to them at every moment. In Malachi 4:6, God promises, "And he will turn the hearts of fathers to their children and the hearts of children to their fathers." By investing our time, attention, and affection in our children, we create lasting bonds of love and trust that will endure for a lifetime.

Fatherhood is a sacred and noble calling, requiring wisdom, strength, and unwavering commitment. As men called to greatness, let us embrace the sacred responsibility of guiding and shaping the next generation, instilling in them the values, virtues, and vision needed to thrive in a world filled with challenges and opportunities. Let us heed the words of Proverbs 20:7, which says, "The righteous who walks in his integrity—blessed are his children after him!" Let us walk in integrity and righteousness, knowing that our example will be a blessing to our children and generations to come.

CHAPTER 9

RESTORING BROKENNESS:
HEALING WOUNDS AND BUILDING BRIDGES

In the journey of life, brokenness stands as a universal experience, a testament to the fragility of the human condition and the inevitability of pain and suffering. But in the midst of brokenness, there is also the opportunity for healing, restoration, and renewal. As men called to greatness, we are tasked with the sacred duty of extending grace, compassion, and forgiveness to ourselves and others and playing a role in the restoration of broken lives and relationships.

The Bible is replete with stories of brokenness and restoration, offering hope and encouragement to all who find themselves in the depths of despair. In Psalm 34:18, we are reminded, "The Lord is near to the brokenhearted and saves the crushed in spirit." This verse speaks to the compassionate nature of our God, who is ever-present in our times of greatest need, offering comfort, solace, and healing to those who are brokenhearted.

But the journey of healing begins with a willingness to acknowledge and confront the brokenness within ourselves. In Psalm 51:17, David writes, "The sacrifices of God are a broken spirit; a broken and contrite heart, O God, you will not despise." This verse reminds us that it is only through humility and repentance that we can experience true healing and restoration in our lives.

One of the greatest barriers to healing is the refusal to forgive—holding onto resentment, bitterness, and anger towards those who have wronged us. In Colossians 3:13, Paul exhorts us, "Bear with each other and forgive one another if any of you has a grievance against someone. Forgive as the Lord forgave you." This verse underscores the importance of extending grace and forgiveness to others, just as we have received forgiveness from God.

But forgiveness does not mean that we condone or excuse the wrongs that have been done to us. Rather, it is a conscious choice to release ourselves from the burden of bitterness and resentment and to extend grace and compassion to those who have hurt us. In Matthew 6:14-15, Jesus says, "For if you forgive other people when they sin against you, your heavenly

Father will also forgive you. But if you do not forgive others their sins, your Father will not forgive your sins." This passage emphasizes the importance of forgiveness in the Christian life and the consequences of withholding forgiveness from others.

Another key aspect of restoring brokenness is the practice of reconciliation—the process of repairing damaged relationships and building bridges of understanding and empathy. In 2 Corinthians 5:18-19, Paul writes, "All this is from God, who reconciled us to himself through Christ and gave us the ministry of reconciliation: that God was reconciling the world to himself in Christ, not counting people's sins against them. And he has committed to us the message of reconciliation." This passage reminds us that we are called to be ambassadors of reconciliation, extending grace and forgiveness to all those we encounter.

Restoring brokenness is a sacred and noble calling, requiring humility, compassion, and unwavering commitment. As men called to greatness, let us extend grace and forgiveness to ourselves and others and play a role in the restoration of broken lives and relationships. Let us heed the words of Isaiah 61:1, which says, "The Spirit of the Sovereign Lord is on me because the Lord has anointed me to proclaim good news to the poor. He has sent me to bind up the brokenhearted, to proclaim freedom for the captives and release from darkness for the prisoners." Let us be instruments of healing and restoration in a world filled with brokenness and pain.

CHAPTER 10

WALKING IN INTEGRITY:
LIVING AUTHENTICALLY
AND WITH PURPOSE

Integrity serves as a foundational piece that stands as the bedrock upon which our character is built, the cornerstone of authenticity and purpose. It is the quality that defines who we are when no one is watching, the measure of our honesty, and the consistency of our actions with our beliefs. As men called to greatness, we are tasked with the sacred duty of walking in integrity, living authentically and with purpose in every aspect of our lives.

The Bible speaks extensively on the importance of integrity, recognizing it as a foundational virtue that leads to success and blessing. In Proverbs 10:9, we are told, "Whoever walks in integrity walks securely, but whoever takes crooked paths will be found out." This verse emphasizes the importance of honesty and consistency in our dealings with others, knowing that integrity brings security and stability to our lives.

However, walking in integrity requires more than just outward conformity to moral standards; it requires a deep-seated commitment to living out our values and beliefs in every area of our lives. In Psalm 15:2, David asks, "Lord, who may dwell in your sacred tent? Who may live on your holy mountain?" The answer, given in verses 2-5, includes characteristics such as speaking the truth from the heart, doing what is right, and keeping one's promises. These qualities exemplify the essence of integrity, demonstrating a life lived in alignment with God's standards.

One of the greatest challenges to walking in integrity is the temptation to compromise our values for the sake of expediency or personal gain. In Proverbs 11:3, we are reminded, "The integrity of the upright guides them, but the unfaithful are destroyed by their duplicity." This verse warns against the dangers of hypocrisy and deceit, urging us to hold fast to our principles even in the face of adversity or temptation.

Integrity is not just about avoiding wrongdoing; it is also about actively doing what is right and honorable in every situation. In Micah 6:8, we are instructed, "He has shown you, O mortal, what is good. And what does the Lord require of you? To act justly and to love mercy and to walk humbly with your God." This verse encapsulates the essence of integrity, calling us to pursue justice, show compassion, and walk in humility in all our interactions with others.

Another key aspect of walking in integrity is the willingness to take responsibility for our actions and make amends when we fall short of our ideals. In Psalm 51:10, David prays, "Create in me a pure heart, O God, and renew a steadfast spirit within me." This prayer reflects a humble acknowledgment of our need for God's grace and forgiveness and a sincere desire to live a life of integrity and authenticity.

Walking in integrity is a lifelong journey of growth and transformation, requiring humility, courage, and unwavering commitment. As men called to greatness, let us strive to live authentically and with purpose, knowing that integrity is the foundation upon which true success and fulfillment are built. Let us heed the words of Proverbs 20:7, which says, "The righteous who walks in his integrity—blessed are his children after him!" Let us walk in integrity and righteousness, leaving a legacy of honor and blessing for generations to come.

CHAPTER 11

THE LEGACY OF LOVE:

LEAVING A LASTING IMPACT
ON THE WORLD

Revisiting my love for music, I emphasize its role as a symphony in parallel life (again) and asserting that love stands as the most powerful and enduring melody, echoing through the corridors of time and shaping the destinies of homes, communities, nations, and dare I say, the world. It is the invisible force with visible effects that binds us together, transcending barriers of time, culture, and circumstance. As men called to greatness, we are tasked with the sacred duty of leaving a legacy of love—a legacy that will endure long after we have passed from this earth and continue to inspire and uplift generations to come.

The Bible speaks eloquently on the subject of love, recognizing it as the greatest of all virtues and the very essence of God's nature. In 1 Corinthians 13:13, Paul writes, "And now these three remain faith, hope, and love. But the greatest of these is love." This verse underscores the centrality of love in the Christian life, affirming its supreme importance above all other qualities.

But love is more than just a feeling or emotion; it is a deliberate choice and a way of life. In John 13:34-35, Jesus commands his disciples, "A new command I give you: Love one another. As I have loved you, so you must love one another. By this, everyone will know that you are my disciples if you love one another." This passage highlights the sacrificial nature of love, calling us to emulate the selfless love that Christ demonstrated during His earthly ministry.

One of the greatest expressions of love is service—the willingness to humble ourselves and put the needs of others above our own. In Mark 10:45, Jesus declares, "For even the Son of Man did not come to be served, but to serve, and to give his life as a ransom for many." This verse exemplifies the selfless love that lies at the heart of Christ's mission and calls us to follow His example by serving others with humility and compassion.

But love is not just about serving those who are easy to love; it is also about extending grace and compassion to those who are difficult or undeserving. In Luke 6:27-28, Jesus says, "But to you who are listening I say: Love your enemies, do good to those who hate you, bless those who curse you, pray for those who mistreat you." This radical teaching challenges us to break free from the cycle of hatred and retaliation and to respond to hostility with love and forgiveness.

Another key aspect of leaving a legacy of love is the importance of investing in relationships—taking the time to nurture and cultivate meaningful connections with those around us. In 1 John 4:7-8, we are reminded, "Beloved, let us love one another, for love is from God, and whoever loves has been born of God and knows God. Anyone who does not love does not know God because God is love." This passage underscores the importance of love as the defining characteristic of our relationship with God and with one another.

The legacy of love is the greatest gift that we can leave to future generations—a gift that transcends time and space and continues to inspire and uplift long after we are gone. As men called to greatness, let us strive to embody the selfless love that Christ demonstrated during His earthly ministry and to leave a lasting impact on the world through acts of compassion, service, and grace. Let us heed the words of 1 Corinthians 16:14, which says, "Let all that you do be done in love." Let us live each day with a heart full of love, knowing that in doing so, we fulfill our divine purpose and leave a legacy that will endure for eternity.

CHAPTER 12

ELEVATING YOUR SPIRIT:
LIVING IN ALIGNMENT
WITH DIVINE CALLING

God has designed our spirits to stand as the beacons of light, helping to guide others towards their divine calling and purpose. It is the essence of who we are, the spark of divinity that animates our being and propels us towards greatness. As men called to fulfill our destiny, we are tasked with the sacred duty of elevating our spirits—of aligning our lives with the higher purpose for which we were created.

The Bible is replete with teachings on the importance of elevating our spirits and living in alignment with our divine calling. In Romans 12:2, we are instructed, "Do not conform to the pattern of this world but be transformed by the renewing of your mind. Then you will be able to test and approve what God's will is—his good, pleasing and perfect will." This verse underscores the importance of aligning our thoughts, words, and actions with the will of God so that we may fulfill our purpose and destiny.

But living in alignment with divine calling requires more than just passive conformity; it requires active engagement and intentional effort. In Proverbs 3:5-6, we are told, "Trust in the Lord with all your heart and lean not on your own understanding; in all your ways submit to him, and he will make your paths straight." This passage reminds us of the importance of surrendering our will to God's guidance and trusting in His wisdom and provision as we navigate the journey of life.

One of the key aspects of elevating our spirits is the cultivation of spiritual disciplines—practices such as prayer, meditation, and study of the Scripture that help us to deepen our connection with the divine. In Matthew 6:6, Jesus instructs us, "But when you pray, go into your room, close the door and pray to your Father, who is unseen. Then your Father, who sees what is done in secret, will reward you." This verse highlights the importance of carving out time for intimate communion with God, away from the distractions of the world.

Spiritual elevation is not just about personal piety; it is also about living out our faith in practical ways that bring glory to God and benefit to others. In James 1:27, we are told, "Religion that God our Father accepts as pure and faultless is this: to look after orphans and widows in their distress and to keep oneself from being polluted by the world." This verse challenges us to embody the love and compassion of Christ in our interactions with others, particularly those who are marginalized or in need.

Another key aspect of living in alignment with the divine calling is the pursuit of excellence—the commitment to giving our best in everything we do as an offering of worship to God. In Colossians 3:23-24, we are reminded, "Whatever you do, work at it with all your heart, as working for the Lord, not for human masters, since you know that you will receive an inheritance from the Lord as a reward. It is the Lord Christ you are serving." This passage underscores the importance of excellence as a reflection of our commitment to honoring God in all areas of our lives.

Elevating your spirit is a lifelong journey of growth and transformation, requiring humility, faith, and unwavering commitment. As men called to fulfill our divine calling, let us strive to align our lives with the higher purpose for which we were created, surrendering our will to God's guidance and living out our faith with passion and excellence. Let us heed the words of Psalm 37:4, which says, "Take delight in the Lord, and he will give you the desires of your heart." Let us delight ourselves in the Lord, knowing that in doing so, we fulfill our divine purpose and bring glory to God.